PRODUCTIVITY AT WORK

36 tricks that will make you better at your job

Written by Robert F. Basil
Illustrations by Jordi Ventura

ISBN: 9781689563741

To my kids Liam and Sophia, without whom this book would have taken a lot less time to write

INTRODUCTION

I just finished writing this book and tucked my kids into bed. But my wife won't let me go to sleep, she insists that the book needs an introduction.

My, oh, my, I love her so much! So I'm gonna be brief.

Being productive is actually pretty easy.

Here you are, you started reading this book. This means that you already have the most important thing: *attitude*. From here on, it's all downhill.

In this book, I've collected 36 productivity tricks. These are no abstract ideas or complex systems: these are little concrete things that will save you time and help you work faster.

All these 36 tricks have proven helpful to me.

I hope they help you too.

1

Use Lightshot for screenshots

If you apply only one trick from the whole book, it should be this one. So, please, pay attention.

Screenshots are very useful. I am constantly sending them by email. To the I.T. dept.: "hey, this button here doesn't work". To the Design dept.: "hey, I would make this image bigger". To the Marketing dept.: "hey, the report is cool but please switch these charts".

Screenshots are painful to take. Here's the whole process:

1. press "Print Screen"
2. open Paint
3. paste the image
4. select the area of interest
5. crop the image to selection
6. click on "Select All"
7. copy
8. switch to the email tab
9. paste the image to the email body.

Booooring!

A lot of steps for an operation that should be simple.

Maybe you use Windows' *"Snipping tool"* instead. It's better, but not by much. Still too many steps.

The tool you need is called Lightshot.

Download it and install it in 30 seconds. Once installed, no need to configure or learn anything.

Here's all you need to know: Lightshot will fire whenever you press "Print Screen".

The screenshotting process becomes quick and intuitive: select the screen area that you are interested in and choose between *copy*, *save*, or *upload to the cloud*.

You can even draw arrows and add text on the spot.

Quick and simple. No more tedious process.

Try Lightshot. You'll wonder why Windows doesn't come with its functionality installed by default. Smarten up, Bill Gates!

You'll find it here: bit.do/lightshot-app

To the Mac users who are thinking "I don't need this": you too should download Lightshot. Apple's screenshotting functionality is better than Windows' but far far faaaar away from Lightshot's.

2

Big flashy headphones prevent interruptions

Some tasks require your full uninterrupted concentration: building a new report template from scratch, analyzing some messy data, writing an important letter to a big client...

For these kinds of tasks, interruptions are productivity killers. When you are interrupted, you lose focus. And it takes your brain 25 minutes to focus again. 25 minutes, even if the interruption lasted only 5 seconds (I didn't make this up, trust me, I read it somewhere*).

An example: a task that would take you 30 minutes to complete becomes 55 minutes with just one interruption. Double the time! If only you could've been left alone for 30 minutes!

But avoiding petty interruptions can be difficult in an office. We've all been there: Sonia asks you for the stapler, Jeff tells you a lame joke, Bob wants to know whether you'll join later for lunch, Laura thanks you for the last report...

...interruption after interruption slowly draining you of your precious time.

Pausing email and chat notifications helps, but you'll still have to deal with face-to-face interruptions. You'll be safe and alone in a meeting room, but there's seldom one available.

Here's a simple but effective trick: buy some big-ass headphones and put them on.

The music will help you concentrate. But, most importantly: people will think twice before interrupting you. That's why *ear*phones don't do the trick: you need big bulky colorful *head*phones so that people notice them.

The flashier, the better.

Putting on headphones is the equivalent of stapling a sign to your forehead that says: "REALLY BUSY HERE". But, unlike the sign, it's not rude.

A note of caution: don't overuse this trick. It's only for when you need 100% sharp focus. Communication in the workplace is important, don't be a loner.

Aha!: bit.do/interruptions

3
The best date format is YYYY-MM-DD

The Japanese invented a lot of good things.

Their best invention, right before sushi, was the YYYY-MM-DD date format. *Year*, followed by *Month*, followed by *Day*. With zero-padding, of course ("*2019-02-01*" instead of "*2019-2-1*").

So elegant! Why is it the best?

- **It can't be misinterpreted.**
  Imagine you read *"6-10-2019"*. Is it *"6th of October"* or *"10th of June"*? Who knows. With the Japanese format instead, *2019-10-06* is clearly the *6th of October* (because it would make no sense to put the day after the year *but* before the month). Say goodbye to misunderstandings.

- **It keeps chronological order when sorted alphabetically.**
  Maybe you're working with Excel, it didn't detect that the cells are dates and it stored them as text. Or maybe you have a folder full of files that contain dates in their names (e.g. "Sales 31-01-2019", "Sales 01-02-2019", etc.). In both cases, if you want to sort chronologically, you are in trouble. You can only sort alphabetically.

When alphabetically ordering text-based dates, the only way to ensure that chronological order is maintained is to use the Japanese YYYY-MM-DD format. Any other format fails.

They invented gunpowder. They invented instant noodles. They invented the YYYY-MM-DD date format. Beware of the Japanese, they are gonna conquer the world.

4

A faster mouse + keyboard shortcuts

Go increase the speed of your computer's mouse. Here's how you do it:

Control Panel > Hardware & Sound > Mouse > Pointer Options > Motion

C'mon, go do it. Now. It will take you only 1 minute to get used to the new speed. You spend 8 hours a day on the computer, most of them with your hand on the mouse. This little boost in productivity quickly adds up.

That being said, whenever possible, you should avoid using the mouse at all. Even at max speed, it is too slow. The keyboard is way better.

Here are some neat keyboard shortcuts to keep your hand off the mouse:

GENERAL

Ctrl + Z & Ctrl + Y	Undo & Redo	Basic
Ctrl + C & Ctrl + V	Copy & Paste	
Ctrl + F	Find *(also in webs!)*	Advanced
Ctrl + Tab	Move through programs	

TEXT

Ctrl + B or U or I	Bold, Underline, Italics	Basic
Alt + arrow	Navigate word by word	
Ctrl + arrow	Navigate by line or by cell	Advanced
Same but + Shift	Select while navigating	
Ctrl + A	Select All	
Ctrl + V + Shift	Paste without formatting	Pro

CHROME

Ctrl + N	Open new window	Basic
Ctrl + T	Open new tab	
Ctrl + click link	Open in new tab	Advanced
Ctrl + L	Go to URL bar	
Ctrl + Shift + T	Open last closed window	Pro

(The last one is awesome! You can use it as many times as you want)

These are the most useful ones. Learn and practice a couple every day, and you'll soon become a keyboard *virtuoso*.

Once you master them all (it will take you no time), go look for more. Keyboard shortcuts are so powerful that they are addictive. You'll learn to hate the mouse so much that you'll end up calling it "the rat".

Footnote for non-English-speakers: Configure all your programs to use English. If you don't, the same function will have different shortcuts in different programs. For example: in Spanish, "Bold" will be Ctrl+N in Excel but Ctrl+B in Gmail... not good!

5

Draw better charts: the basics

Data is very important for business. Without it, you can't make good decisions.

But data is often complex and difficult to read. That's why we invented charts: to be able to interpret complex data at a glance.

Nowadays, with Excel, it's easy for you to draw charts. But if you don't put some thought into it, you're gonna end up with crappy charts.

Crappy charts hide the data, take a lot of time to understand, and mislead. Good charts highlight the data, are understood at a glance, and inform.

Let me show you an example.

CRAPPY CHART

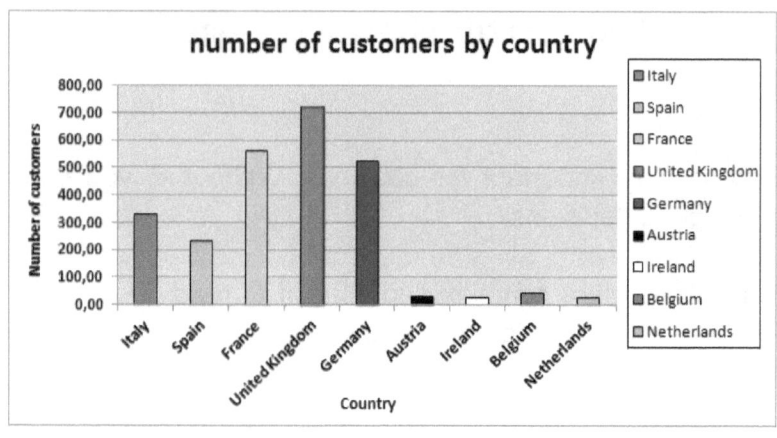

DON'T

- Repeat information
  Like labels. It distracts the eye

- Slant text
  Slanted and vertical texts are hard to read

- Use unnecessary colors
  Color is distracting

- Use unnecessary precision
  Mind the number of decimals and the size of axis intervals

- Overuse bold text

GOOD CHART

Customer Base
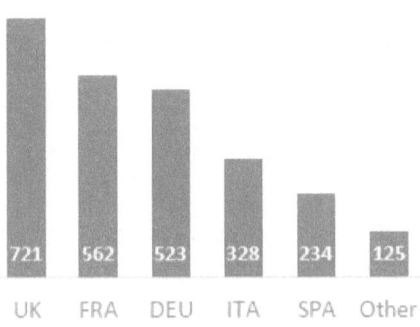

(as of 2020-04-01)

721	562	523	328	234	125
UK	FRA	DEU	ITA	SPA	Other

DO

- Sort the data
  See? Now you can see the ranking at a glance

- Remove clutter
  Like borders, gridlines, background and redundant labels

- Use colors only when needed
  Color is distracting

- Lighten and gray secondary elements
  Like labels, axes and lines

- Write a short descriptive title

- Choose thoughtful intervals for axes
  Or remove axes if you can label directly

- Align text horizontally
  Use common abbreviations

15

See how much the chart improved? Even though it has more information, it is a lot less crowded.

The general idea is to remove everything that is not data so that data can stand out.

To draw even better charts with some advanced techniques, check chapter 12.

DIVE DEEPER:
A book that will change the way you think of charts:
bit.do/visual-display

6

Create a "DELETE" folder

Sometimes you need to create temporary files. I'm talking about files that, at the very moment of creation, you already know you will delete right after.

This happens mostly with files you create just to email them to someone: a screenshot, a pdf conversion of a doc file, a watered-down version of an Excel report. It also happens with files that you create to quickly test some calculations or draft a text.

If you are anything like me, you usually forget to delete these temporary files. They end up cluttering your computer and taking a lot of your hard drive's memory.

This is not good. This is bad. But there's an easy fix.

Create a new folder in your desktop and call it "DELETE". Whenever you find yourself creating a temporary file, save it there.

This way, even if you forget to delete the file right after using it, you'll be able to periodically get rid of ALL the dead files at once. No more file-hunting expeditions.

For the "DELETE" folder to be easy to access from the "Save" inspector window, it has to be on your desktop.

Name the folder whatever you want. One of my friends named it "GARGANTUA", and another one "THE PIT OF DEATH" (This is Spartaaaa!). Mine is "MORDOR" (what can I say? I love *Lord of the Rings*). As long as you create the folder, I'm happy with whatever name you choose.

7

Follow this screw-up protocol

No matter how good you are at what you do, you're gonna screw it up one day. And another day. And yet another one.

If you're good (and you'll sure be, after reading this book ;)), it won't happen often. But I assure you that it's going to happen every now and then.

Maybe you sent an unfinished email to all the newsletter subscribers. Maybe you inadvertently messed up a database. Maybe you ordered the wrong materials for the event next week. Silly mistakes that cost money to the company.

When you screw it up, don't panic.

You just made a mistake. We all do. It's understandable.

Don't try to hide it. It's gonna surface someday (and even if it doesn't, the fear that it might will eat you alive).

Don't try to blame it on someone else. It's unfair and you're better than that.

When you screw it up, follow a simple protocol:

- **SOLVE IT:** before it gets worse. If you can't solve it yourself, contact the appropriate person.
- **REPORT IT:** to your boss and whoever else is affected.
- **OWN IT:** clearly state that it's your fault (but don't overdo it, this is no public execution).
- **PUT PREVENTIONS IN PLACE:** to stop it from happening again.

It is that simple. As soon as you solved the issue, send a short email:

> Hi,
>
> our subscribers have received this month's newsletter and all the links were broken. It was my responsibility to review it.
>
> I've already sent them a second email with the links fixed, apologizing.
>
> From now on, the final check will be done by both Alicia and me. We've also established that we'll always send first a 1.000-email batch and 30 minutes later, if everything seems right, send the rest.
>
> Thanks,

We all make mistakes. What sets us apart is how we react to them.

If you make a mistake but follow this protocol afterwards, your boss will trust you even more than if you hadn't made the mistake in the first place. Next time, remember: solve it, report it, own it and put preventions in place.

8

Writing Well: 2 misconceptions

Writing well is the single most important skill to master if you want to become a productive worker.

It saves time and money. Hell of a lot of it.

No one ever taught you how to write well. Don't worry, I'll do it in 2 chapters (chapters 14 and 22).

But first, you need a reset. Know that:

- **Writing is *not* an art, writing is a craft.**
  Everyone can learn to write well, it only takes effort and practice.

- **There are no good writers, only good rewriters.**
  As Hemingway said, *"The first draft of anything is shit"*. Rewrite, rewrite, and rewrite.

That's the trick: unlearn these two mistaken ideas about writing. This alone will already make you a better (re)writer.

DIVE DEEPER:
Become a better writer overnight: bit.do/scott-adams
Good writing is clear, simple, concise and human:
bit.do/on-writing-well

9

Improve your Google searches

The internet is vast. So vast, it is sometimes difficult to find what you are looking for. Thank God we have Google.

Or, better yet, thank Larry Page and Sergey Brin.

When Larry and Sergey created Google, they made the world a huge favor. What a wonder!: the world's information readily available at your fingertips.

But there's so much to Google Search that you don't know about! These tricks will help you make the most of Google's capabilities. Use:

- **Quotes** (" ") to search for an exact phrase
  "Connected Consumer Survey 2018-2019"

- **Asterisk** (*) within quotes as "any word/s" wildcard
  "Connected * Survey"

- **Minus sign** (-) to exclude words
  buy mouse -computer -gaming

- **site:** to search in a specific web
  yourCompanyName site:reddit.com

In general:

- **Use only the essential words**

  "Excel date difference" instead of "Microsoft Excel how to calculate the difference between two dates".

- **Remember to be specific**

  Don't type "event London", type "event agency London" instead.

- **Use synonyms when you're not getting what you want**

  If "twilight" only gives you hormonal vampire pics, try "sunset".

Larry and Sergey put a lot of effort into making Google the best search engine out there. Every time you make a lousy Google search, they both burst into tears. Make them happy by using these tricks.

10

Clean up your computer's desktop

Stop reading for a moment and have a look at your computer's screen. Count the number of icons in your desktop (including folders, program shortcuts, documents, files, recycling bin... everything).

If you have more than 10, you have too many. Your desktop is too crowded, and it's making your computer run slow.

So go ahead and clean it up.

It's easy:

- Delete all the program shortcuts that you don't use often.

- Move all the files to folders.

- Convert into subfolders the folders that you don't access often.

- Delete or sort into folders all your other junk.

Here's a representative before and after picture:

BEFORE   **AFTER**

Thanks to trick #10, Albert's desktop lost 20 pounds in just 5 minutes.
Try it now for free!

Cleaning up the desktop cuts down your computer's RAM usage and makes it run a lot faster.

But this trick won't only make your computer run faster, it will also make *you* run faster. When things are sorted, they are way easier to find.

11

When asking, polite but to the point

When dealing with other people, it is important to remember that, well… they are *people*.

In the heat of the moment, we sometimes forget it and treat people like robots. Dry and impersonal. Or we do the exact opposite: we waste time on niceties (remember that this is the workplace, efficiency is paramount).

Find the right tone, especially when writing emails. It depends a little bit on your personality, but there are clear dos and don'ts:

Hi, send me the sales report.

Too dry

Hi, I need the sales report.

Hi, can you send me the sales report?
Thanks

Good

Hi, could you send me the sales report?
Thanks

Perfect

Hi, could you send me the sales report please? Thanks	Good

Hi, could you send me the sales report please? Thank you very much Hi, I know that you are very busy but, if it's not a problem, could you please send me the sales report? I really need it. Thank you very much.	Too nice

You are looking for "kind and professional", that's where the sweet spot is. Polite but to the point.

There are many ways to achieve it. My choice: I use the conditional tense ("could" instead of "can"), add a "thanks", and spare the "please".

Find your tone and stick to it in all communications (email, chat, face to face) with people in all positions (from intern to CEO).

You can of course add a brief joke every now and then. A little party never killed nobody.

12

Draw better charts: cool techniques

If you want to impress people with your charts (who wouldn't?), learn these cool techniques:

Replace pie charts with column charts

Columns are easier to compare than areas and allow for an extra layer of data (targets, in the example).

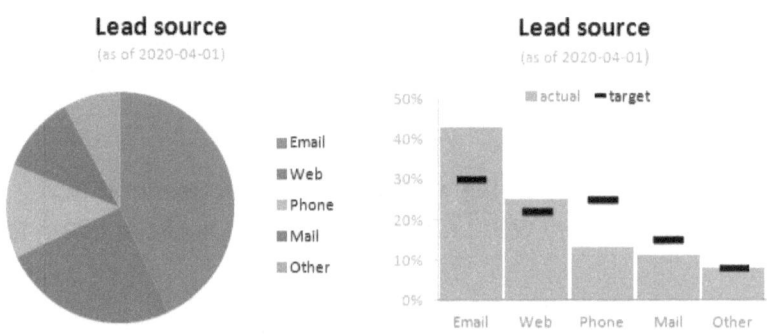

HOW TO: Sort the data, Choose "Columns" chart type, Add new Series, Right click on new columns, Change chart type.

Mark significant events with text and pointers
Tell a story through the chart.

Unique Visitors
(as of 2020-01-01)

HOW TO: Add a textbox and a line, but do it with the chart selected so that if you move the chart they move along with it.

Label directly on the data (instead of legend)
Choose color and position wisely.

Market Share

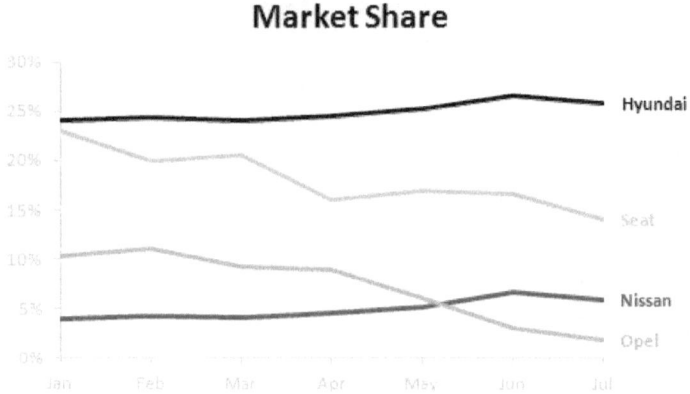

Performance

HOW TO: Right click on data, Add data label.

Use lighter colors or dotted lines for projections and incomplete data
It's a quick way to warn the reader.

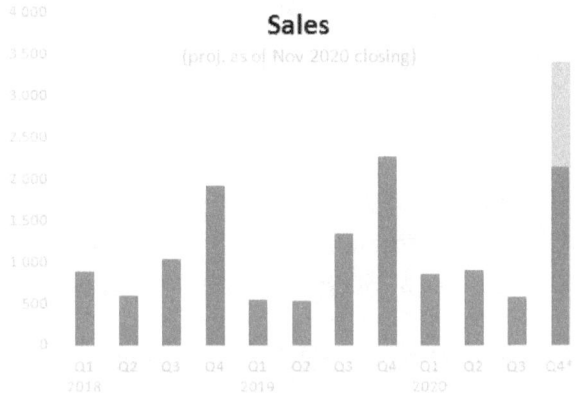

HOW TO: Add a new series with the same values + the projection, Right click on the columns, set Series Overlap to 100%. Another option: Use a stacked column chart.

Write dynamic titles
Ideal for reports that need to be updated periodically.

	fx	=D2&" Sales"				
C		D	E	F		G
Current Month:		April	4 000			
Chart title:		April Sales		**April Sales**		
			3 500			

HOW TO: Select the chart title, Click on the formula bar, Type =, Select a cell with the appropriate formula in it, Hit Enter.

13

Your boss has to decide.
What info will she need?

At work, you can't always decide everything. Sometimes, your job is to just gather information and the final decision is the responsibility of your boss. So you leave it to her.

That's good. Let's face it: she probably knows better.

Here's an example: your company will launch a new product. Your boss, the head of the Marketing department, has asked you to come up with ideas for a marketing campaign.

So you work on it for a couple of days and boil it down to 3 options. You then go to her, present the 3 options, and ask her: "Alright, which one do you prefer?"

Sneaky little bastard, you already know what comes next: she starts asking more and more questions:

> *I see you computed the cost of each campaign, but... how many people is each campaign going to impact? Are the target audiences the same? Do all the campaigns take the same amount of time to execute? What number of sales can we expect? Have we done something similar in the past? What were the results?*

A lot of questions means more work for you. You'll have to go back to your desk and continue gathering information.

It's frustrating. Why is she always like this? Why does she have to order more work? Can't she just decide?

Well, NO. Of course she can't decide. How could she? It's not that she enjoys loading you with more work, it's just that you didn't give her the *relevant* information.

And it's your fault. You should've known better. You rushed to do the work without stopping to think for a minute.

Here's what you should've done instead: before asking your boss for a decision, *always* ask yourself: what info will she need to decide? Put yourself in her shoes: if you were in charge of deciding, what would you need to know to make a good decision?

Then gather this info, summarize it, and present it to your boss.

The extra step of stopping to think will take you only 5 minutes. And it will save you way more than that in unnecessary back-and-forths.

Granted, you'll still forget things. But not as many, and even fewer as you get some practice and start thinking like your boss (time for a promotion?).

14

Writing Well: 7 simple rules

No matter whether you are writing a formal report or a relaxed email, be sure to:

Keep your sentences short
Don't put multiple thoughts in a sentence. Use fewer commas and more periods.

> The event, that was held the 23rd of May and took a lot of work to organize, ended up being a disaster.

> The event took a lot of work to organize. It was held the 23rd of May. It was a disaster.

Use short words

> The objective is to utilize incentivization only in the conclusion.

> The goal is to use rewards only in the end.

Remove unnecessary words

> It is of course very important to pay close attention.

> It is important to pay attention.

Mind the order of the words
Related things must go together.

> The event was planned by the whole team in Los Angeles.

> The event in Los Angeles was planned by the whole team.

Avoid the passive voice
The active voice (Subject-Verb-Object) is easier for readers to understand.

The event was planned by the Marketing dept. It was attended by a lot of people.

■ The Marketing dept. planned the event. A lot of people attended.

Be direct
Own your opinions and don't show doubt.

I think that maybe next time it will be better if we play some music.

■ We should play some music next time.

Give examples
Examples help people understand. Don't tell, show.

The event was a disaster because the cost was higher than usual and the attendance was lower than expected. Paul shared his impression with us and it was not good.

■ The event was a disaster: it cost $10,000 and only 9 people showed up. Paul said "Shitty results, never again".

DIVE DEEPER:
A great book on writing (chapter 5.4 alone already justifies buying it): bit.do/100-ways

A classic: bit.do/elements-of-style

15

TL;DR is the new executive summary

When writing, always aim for short. Short is better.

But, sometimes, short is not possible. Some topics call for detail, and detail is inherently long. When you absolutely need to extend, extend.

Then you have a problem: people don't like to read. Reading takes a lot of time. When presented with a long text (a lengthy email, a 2-page report), people don't know if it's worth their time.

The solution? Add a TL;DR at the top.

TL;DR stands for "Too Long; Didn't Read", and it's just a modern synonym for the old plain "executive summary": a short paragraph that summarizes the content below.

Putting it at the top of your document makes it easy for people to know what's in it and to decide whether they should dive deeper.

Whenever you write something longer than 3 paragraphs, make sure to add a TL;DR at the top. No matter how long the text, don't make the TL;DR longer than 6 sentences.

When I'm writing my TL;DRs, I like to imagine that I'm writing a telegraph. Nothing is superfluous, every word counts.

For example, for a 10-page report:

> **TL;DR:** Sales -20% QoQ. Discarded causes: price, sales training, marketing reach. Possible cause: confusing new promo. Solution: go back to Q2's promo scheme (Cost: $14,500, ready by 04-14, Goal: +35% sales MoM).

here would follow the actual 10-page report, with details like:

- When and where sales dropped
- Why you discarded some causes
- What makes the new promo problematic
- Why Q2's promo was better
- Steps necessary to switch back to Q2's promo

- Detailed costs of the change
- Calculations for the new sales forecast
- Timeline of the changes
- Prayer to the ancient gods for sales to go up

Footnote: you can find the TL;DRs for this book's chapters on page 86. Notice that they include only the essence. No explanations, no examples, no digressions. Just the bare minimum to understand what we are talking about.

16

Shorten meetings by
stacking them one after the other

Meetings are time suckers. And you attend too many. Most of the times, a 1-hour meeting could've been just an email.

You should avoid meetings at all costs. Don't be afraid to reject an invitation if you deem it unnecessary.

But even when a meeting is justified or unavoidable, it tends to take too much of your time. It starts too late and goes on for too long.

Here's a little trick to shorten your meetings: whenever possible, stack all of them one after the other.

Make them public in your calendar, so people know. Announce it when you are entering the room: "Hey, I have another meeting in 30 minutes, I hope this won't be a problem". Warn 10 minutes before the meeting's scheduled end: "Hey, I have only 10 minutes left, let's wrap this up".

This trick can cause some problems in the beginning (you'll miss some meetings, what a big problem...) but in the long run people will get used to it and they'll feel forced to respect your time. Believe me, this system will pay off.

I'd love to develop this explanation further but, I'm sorry, I have a meeting in 2 minutes. See ya!

17

On office hours
and counting the minutes

When it comes to managing office hours, every company is different. Flexible working hours, different arrival and departure times, short or long lunch breaks, optional remote-work days, personal hours leave...

Whatever your company's official policy, there are 3 personal rules you should follow:

- **Always be on time.** Punctuality is important.

- **Always keep the same schedule** so that people know when they can count on you being at the office. "Schedule" includes everything: entry time, lunchtime and remote-work day (e.g. always on Wednesdays).

- **Never discount the minutes.** If today you arrived 10 minutes earlier or ate 20 minutes quicker, well, good for you. But the company doesn't owe you anything. Don't leave the office early. Skimping minutes is unprofessional and will make you miserable.
    - This rule doesn't apply when it goes against you: if you arrived 5 minutes late, leave 5 minutes later. If you took a 24-minute break for personal matters, make up for these 24 minutes (during lunchtime, for example).

Follow these rules without questioning day in, day out. Your life will be easier. Tell me, don't you want an easier life?

18

Boomerang for those who don't reply

Let's imagine your boss asked you for a new report. He needs it in 2 weeks.

You quickly complete the first part of the report, but then you need some more data to continue. Only Joe from I.T. can gather this data, so you send him an email. You are a good person and Joe is trustworthy. So you give him a reasonable deadline and trust that you'll hear back from him. You move on to other tasks and forget about the report.

Flash forward to 2 weeks later: well, Joe didn't see the email. You never heard back from him. It slipped your mind, and here you are: trying to justify it to your boss (good luck!). The report is not done.

None of this would've happened if YOU had installed Boomerang:

REMIND ME IF I DON'T HEAR BACK
With Boomerang, once you send an email you can set a reminder ("if Joe doesn't reply in two days, please remind me"). Sleep tight: everything is gonna be alright.

None of this would've happened if JOE had installed Boomerang:

FOLLOW-UP REMINDERS
With Boomerang, you can also set follow-up reminders on emails you *receive*. When Joe received the data request, he could've said: "hey Boomerang, I don't have time for this now, but please put this email back at the top of my inbox tomorrow at 3 p.m.".

A tool with two simple features that have saved me of many troubles.

Free and easy to install:

Gmail: bit.do/boomerang-gmail
Outlook: bit.do/boomerang-outlook

Disclaimer: I have no affiliation with Boomerang and I get nothing in return for recommending it. It's just a tool that I love.
Footnote to the disclaimer: hey, if you work for Boomerang, hit me up. I'm sure we can work something out ;)

19

Email a Weekly Status Report to your boss

Every Friday, before leaving for your hard-earned joy-filled weekend, take 5 minutes to write a quick email to your boss.

This email is the Weekly Status Report, where you tell her:

- The tasks that you've completed this week.

- The progress you've made on currently ongoing tasks (plus their estimated time to completion).

- The pending tasks planned for next week.

The email should be a bullet list with no more than 8 items. Focus on the highlights.

Do not include petty periodic tasks she already knows about ("I wrote and sent the weekly sales report") unless something significant happened this week ("weekly sales report took 2 more days to write because of the new B.I. System").

Hi Sophie,

Progress made this week:
- <u>New brochures</u>: I wrote all the copy. linkToContent.com.
- <u>B.I. System improvements</u>: I sent our requests to I.T. They agreed to reply by Wed 06-24.
- <u>"Software Solutions" Congress</u>: attended on Tue 06-23. I would like to discuss some ideas with you. Notes: linkToNotesInDrive.com.
- <u>New events team training</u>: I met with both internal sales teams and trained them.

Plan for next week:
- <u>New brochures</u>: request art and send to print.
- <u>Event training</u>: video call with overseas team Wed 07-01 15:00h.
- <u>Monthly Marketing Report</u>: Thursday and Friday will be entirely devoted to writing it. Ready by Friday EOB.

Have a nice weekend! I'm going to the Imagine Dragons concert, I'm sure I'll have as much fun as I had in the 2 sales training sessions… :)

Writing the email will help you keep track of your progress and plan for the next week. And even if your boss doesn't read it, she'll know that you have everything under control.

How about you start this Friday?

20

Become an Excel Ninja
with just 6 functions

You probably have a colleague that dominates Microsoft Excel (or Google Spreadsheets, for that matter).

No matter how difficult the task at hand, he builds a spreadsheet that automatically completes it. For you, seeing him use Excel is like seeing a shaman summon a spirit. Wizardry. Something short of miraculous.

You'd love to be like him. It would make your life so much easier. But some time ago you tried and failed. Microsoft Excel is scary, full of complicated features and impossible to learn.

Let me tell you a secret: 90% of the time, Microsoft Excel is just 6 functions. Learn how to use them and you'll become a shaman:

- IF
- VLOOKUP
- CONCATENATE (aka "&")
- SUMIFS (and COUNTIFS)
- LEN
- LEFT (and RIGHT)

Go visit bit.do/excel-functions and learn how these functions work. In no time, you'll be using them everywhere.

Once you master the functions, explore the cool ways you can combine them in a single formula. For example, can you guess what these formulas do?:

=IF(LEFT(A1, 6)="North-"), VLOOKUP(A1, "database", AA:CC, 0), "unavailable data")

=VLOOKUP(A1&B1&C1, "all_sales"!AA:CC, 4, 0)
(A1&A2&A3 could be a unique identifier like 'sam_august_productA')

=IF(SUMIFS(C2:C9,B2:B9,"<>Free Sample",A2:A9,"Jim") > 100, "ok", "underperforming")

Google Spreadsheets has the same functions and they work the same way: bit.do/g-spreadsheets

Pro-tip: start formulas with "+" instead of "=", it's faster to type.

21

Busy?
Book a meeting with yourself

Working in an office is not easy. New tasks keep coming all the time (an urgent report, a meeting invitation, a request from another department, a PR mini-crisis). You are always busy but the real work (the one that actually brings value) keeps being put off.

It's like you are not in control of your own time. You are not the one managing it and distributing it among the tasks you know are important. The ones that you got hired to do.

That's why a lot of people stay after-hours. The office is empty and the email inbox is quiet: perfect time to get stuff done.

But it doesn't need to be this way. It shouldn't.

Whenever there's something important and you need to devote some time to it, apply this simple trick: book a meeting with yourself in the calendar.

Booking time slots for yourself is a great way to set aside some time for important tasks. It has the extra benefit of serving as a reminder.

So, please, book meetings with yourself often. Remember to set their visibility to "Public" in the calendar.

You are the owner of your time, don't feel ashamed to use it. Take back control.

22

Writing Well: Cut these phrases

You use waaaay more words than you need. In reports, because you wanna sound more professional. In emails, because you wanna look nice.

It doesn't work. Prune your texts.

Here are some commonly used unnecessary words:

Instead of saying...	Say...
very Results are *very good* so far	**eq. adj. (or —)** Results are *great* so far
really They *really* liked it	**eq. verb (or —)** They *loved* it
in order to We did it *in order to* increase sales	**to** We did it *to* increase sales
the truth is that *The truth is that* this book is cool	**—** This book is cool (oh... thanks!)
due to the fact that We cancelled *due to the fact that* it rained	**because** We cancelled *because* it rained
what I would like to say is *What I would like to say is that* we don't need to change	**—** We don't need to change

Instead of saying...	Say...
Let it be said	**—**
Let it be said that we are not against...	We are not against...
It should be pointed out	**—**
It should be pointed out that this was the worst month	This was the worst month
Of course	**—**
We can *of course* change it, but...	We can change it, but...
The present situation advises	**should**
The present situation advises that we stop	We *should* stop
I'd like to start by	**—**
I'd like to start by thanking you all	Thank you all
with the purpose of	**to**
With the purpose of increasing sales...	*To* increase sales...

"In an effort to", "with the aim of", "all of", "send by email", "I'm only gonna say that", "it appears that"... the list could go on forever, you get my point.

Be blunt. Remember: if a word is not indispensable, it doesn't belong there.

I'd like to finish by saying that you must remember that it is of course very important to ensure that your texts are really short in order to facilitate their understanding, as previously mentioned.

23

Look it up before asking for it (and never ask twice)

We humans are by nature lazy. When we need something, we don't bother figuring how to get it ourselves and we go ask someone for it.

Here's a silly example: if you've worked at an office, you've heard people asking *"what time is it?"* They have it there, on the lower right corner of their computer's screen (in front of them!). They have it there, on their phones (in their pocket!).

But they still ask for it.

The *"what time is it"* example is baloney, sure. But we do the same with countless other not so *"oh sorry i'm so stupid"* things.

We ask for documents that we already have in our inboxes. Definitions that we can google. Data that we can get from the department's online repository. And telephone numbers that we can find in the company's shared phone list (or in the signature of the email that the guy sent us last week).

When you do this, you are wasting not only other people's time but also yours.

So, please, the next time you need something, fight the natural instinct to just ask someone for it. Make it a habit to spend 5 seconds wondering *"is there a way that I can get this myself?".*

You'll be amazed by the number of times the answer is *"ouch, of course, yeah!".*

A note of caution: if you can't get something yourself, don't sweat it. Go ahead and ask someone for it. No problem. But here's one thing to remember: if you might need it again in the future, please save it somewhere.

24

The "I have low battery" trick
to shorten phone conversations

When speaking on the phone, it's easy for people to get distracted and let time fly. People love to talk, especially about the same topic again and again. They could do it forever.

Don't get me wrong: that's alright for personal calls. But what's the point of letting a work phone call drag on? It's boring, frustrating and, most of all, inefficient. You have other work to do.

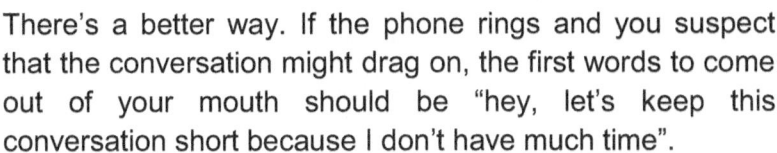

To avoid unnecessarily long calls, you could of course not pick up the phone. That's rude and unprofessional. And, believe me, he's gonna keep calling anyway.

There's a better way. If the phone rings and you suspect that the conversation might drag on, the first words to come out of your mouth should be "hey, let's keep this conversation short because I don't have much time".

If you need this trick often, learn some variations:

- Hey, my battery is dying, let's keep this short.
- Hey, I've got a meeting in 3 minutes, let's make this quick.
- Hey, you caught me in the middle of something but I really want to solve this, help me make it short.

Use this trick for a while and people will get used to going straight to the point when talking to you over the phone.

25

Chat: when you greet, state what you need

Chat is very intrusive. When someone is focused on a task, being distracted by a new chat pop-up (plus a beeping sound) is annoying.

But chat is sometimes necessary. If you need something and you need it now, an email won't do.

Let's say you work in the HR department. Janice from Sales forgot to send you the commissions report, and you already asked for it by email. Twice. If you don't get it this afternoon, you won't have time to close the month*.

It's alright to send her a chat message. But, please, make it quick.

If you start with a:

> Hey Janice!

she'll be distracted by a chat pop-up and stop doing whatever she was doing.

You'll then spend 30 seconds typing your request (because of course you've read this book and you know that, when writing, it is important to be precise).

30 seconds of Janice's precious life.

30 looong seconds that she spent staring at the corner of her screen, waiting for you...

... typing

No wonder Janice looks at you with contempt when you cross paths in the corridor. She doesn't like you. She's fed up with you wasting her time.

The next time you need something from Janice, add the request in the very first message, the one where you greet her. You'll come as polite and professional.

> Hey Janice! Can you please send me the Commissions Report? I need it before 15:00h today to include it in this month's closing. Thank you!

> (Janice knows that "commissions not included in the closing" means "not being paid until next month")

*hey, maybe plan better next time.

26

Your boss is not a robot

Having a good relationship with your boss is important. It will make both of you happier, and it will make your job a lot easier.

Your boss is tired of dealing with kiss-asses and people who are afraid of her. What you should do instead is:

- **BE HONEST:** don't be afraid to speak up when you disagree. Do you think she chose the worst flyer design? Tell her! As long as you do it privately, state your arguments, and respect her authority (she gets to decide), you'll be fine.

- **BE APPROACHABLE:** don't hide what makes you human. Did you have an awesome weekend camping? You can tell her. Going through a rough time at home? Don't be afraid to mention it. Do you fancy Alex from the Finance department? Ok... maybe not *that* approachable.

- **BE PLAYFUL:** acting serious doesn't make you any more professional. Crack a joke or tease her every now and then. A little humor never killed nobody.

In summary: be human. Remember that your boss is not a robot. She is a person, just like you. With her stressful life, her insecurities, and her boss pissing her off every now and then.

So loosen up. Who knows, you might even become friends.

DIVE DEEPER:
A speech that changed my life: bit.do/this-is-water

27

Text formatting was made to be used

Here's a way to keep your texts short and easy to read: make intensive use of bold, italics, underlining, indentation and bullet points.

Compare these 2 emails:

Hi,

this project is quite big, so we had a meeting to distribute the tasks among the team.

In said meeting we agreed that John will take care of the logistics, which must be ready by 06-23. We also decided that the preparation of the new reporting template will be the responsibility of Jennifer, who should have it by 06-23. Last but not least, Hannah will contact the attendants on 06-30.

I will manage the project's coordination. Remember to upload all the files to the department's folder after Laura's revision, it is very important.

Thank you all,

> ## DO
>
> Hi,
>
> **distribution of tasks** as per agreed in the meeting:
>
> - **JOHN:** logistics *(ready by 06-23)*
> - **JENNIFER:** reporting template *(06-23)*
> - **HANNAH:** contact attendants *(06-30)*
> - **ROBERT:** coordination
>
> Upload all the files to the department's folder after Laura's revision.
>
> Thank you all,

Both emails have the same information. Which one is easier to read?

When a piece of text is properly formatted, people can quickly scan through it. Good format makes the text easier to understand.

Formatted text is also easier to write. You write it faster because you don't need to figure out the hard stuff: what sentence connectors to use and how to grammatically highlight the important things. Bullet points and bolding to the rescue!

With the help of formatting, writing feels easy. It's like becoming Shakespeare* overnight.

Use bold, italics, underlining, indentation and bullet points everywhere: reports, emails... even Excel files!

It's for free.

*Pro-tip: remember to use keyboard shortcuts: Ctrl+**B**, Ctrl+**I**, Ctrl+**U**. Notice the pattern?* **B**old, **I**talics, **U**nderline.

*I know that technically speaking Shakespeare was not a writer, he was a poet and playwright. But, c'mon, you get my point.

28

Excel:
3 allies for when a ninja won't do

Ok, so you read chapter 20 and now you are an Excel ninja. But there are times when even a ninja won't do. After all, ninjas ended up losing to the samurais*.

How can you improve your Excel skills?

Do not shove long boring tutorials down your throat. Most of what they teach has no use for your specific needs. And even when it has, you'll have forgotten it by the time you need it.

Don't learn anything unless you need it *now*. The best way to keep learning Excel is to do it while working.

The best sources of Excel knowledge are:

- **GOOGLE:** ideal for doubts on how to solve specific problems. Search things like "Excel difference between two dates" (subtraction or DATEDIF), "Excel round number" (ROUND, duh!) and "Excel dynamic cell reference" (INDIRECT).

- **YOUR COLLEAGUES:** people are eager to teach what they know, don't be afraid to ask. Go to your colleagues for help whenever you:

    - Want to do something but don't even know where to start.
    - Are getting no errors but the results are wrong and you can't see why.
    - Have to deal with data formats particular to your company.

- **INTERNAL COMPANY REPORTS:** whenever you consult a report that has been built with Excel, explore its inner workings. Some guy built it, what functions did he use? How did he organize the data? Tinkering with other people's files is how I discovered cool functions like TRIM, WEEKDAY and EOMONTH and function combinations like VLOOKUP with MATCH.

The most important thing to keep in mind is that:

with Excel, there's always a way.

If you catch yourself doing repetitive operations, too much copy-pasting, or a lot of manual work, stop. Think a little bit: is there a faster way? Resort to Google, your colleagues, and your colleague's reports.

not really. A little artistic license there.

29

Don't name your file "John"

Go to a crowd and shout "Hey John!": a lot of people will turn around. It turns out that there's a lot of people called "John". It is a lot easier to find your friend "Ezequiel".

Names are important. Names need to be specific.

If you name your computer file the equivalent of "John", you'll have a hard time when searching for it some days later. You want to always be looking for Ezequiels.

There are a lot of "John"'s for files, names that say almost nothing about the contents of the file. Here are some: Results, Sales, Analysis, Report, Test.

When naming your files, be specific. Don't save as *"Campaign analysis.xlsx"*, save as *"2019-07-01 Summer Mailing Campaign results analysis.xlsx"* instead.

A trick to come up with specific and unique names is to always add the date. *"Sales 2019-10"* is a lot more informative than just *"Sales"*.

Oh, and never rely solely on the folders' hierarchy to identify a file. It's not enough. A file inside the folder *"Reports > 2019 > October > Sales.xlsx"* becomes unidentifiable once you email it. And it is also difficult to find with the search inspector.

Files accumulate fast. Searching for the final report on that awesome marketing campaign you did last year can be a pain in the ass. A second spent today thinking of a good name for your file is 10 minutes saved tomorrow when looking for it.

30

Search your inbox like a master

Your inbox is probably clogged with emails. Like Diogenes*, you love accumulating everything.

Now, let's suppose you need an email you received some months ago. You know it's there, sitting somewhere in your inbox.

Well... good luck finding it! Needle in a haystack.

There are 2 common solutions to this problem. None works:

DON'T

- Always delete the emails that you won't need (we are assuming that you can predict the future. Can't you??).

- Use the email's tag or folder systems (and end up with 10 haystacks instead of just one).

Both solutions are bad. Even if they worked (they don't), they would take too much time to implement. Time is valuable.

There's only one solution to the needle in a haystack problem: go get a powerful magnet and learn how to use it. In this specific scenario, the "magnet" is the email's search engine.

Learn how to use it with a few simple tricks:
(Note that you can combine many in a single search)

GMAIL

- **from:**peter@awesomeprovider.com
  (also works with to:, cc: and bcc:)

- **has:**attachment
  (also works with :drive, :document, :spreadsheet)

- **before:**2004/04/16 *(use your date format)*
  (also works with after:)

- "Main summer event" looks for emails with the exact phrase in quotes

OUTLOOK

- **from:**peter@awesomeprovider.com
  (also works with to:, cc: and bcc:)

- **hasattachment:**true

- **before:**2004/04/16 *(use your date format)*
  (also works with after: and :thisweek, :thismonth)

- "Main summer event" looks for emails with the exact phrase in quotes

Storage space is virtually free nowadays, so why bother deleting emails? You are only ever gonna need a tiny fraction of your emails, so why bother tagging and sorting them all?

Learn how to search your inbox. Isn't it reassuring to know that everything is archived in case you ever need it again?

Ehem... I thought that adding a Classic Greece reference would make me look smart. Did it work?

31

Draw better data tables

When drawing data tables, people just pile all the numbers together, keep the default formatting on, and call it a day. Are the resulting tables any good?

No, they aren't.

Tables are as important as charts, yet no one puts any effort into drawing them.

Like I did with charts, let me show you an example.

CRAPPY TABLE

Performance by Region and Product						
Region	Product	Launch Date	Sales	Revenue actual	Revenue BP	Goal achievement
North	TOTAL		5828	$ 186820,05	$ 179500	104,1%
North	Albestros	1/9/2019	925	$ 20345,22	$ 22000	92,5%
North	Bartom	15/10/2018	695	$ 10425,52	$ 14500	71,9%
North	Calzari	14/01/2018	2718	$ 81526,01	$ 71000	114,8%
North	Diartond	5/9/2017	1490	$ 74523,3	$ 72000	103,5%
South	TOTAL		10992	$ 320670,43	$ 320700	100,0%
South	Albestros	1/7/2019	1889	$ 41568,32	$ 41500	100,2%
South	Bartom	13/10/2018	2353	$ 35287,84	$ 39000	90,5%
South	Calzari	19/1/2018	4685	$ 140555,84	$ 138000	101,9%
South	Diartond	1/9/2017	2065	$ 103258,43	$ 102200	101,0%
TOTAL	TOTAL		16820	$ 507490,48	$ 500200	101,5%

DON'T

- Draw a thick-lined grid
  White space is usually enough to direct the eye

- Include unnecessary information
  If the launch dates are useful but secondary, de-emphasize

- Use unnecessary precision
  Are these dollar cents relevant?

- Use unnecessary colors
  Color is distracting

- Overuse bold text
  When everything stands out, nothing stands out

GOOD TABLE

		Launch	Sales	$ (actual) ▾	$ (target)	achiev.
South			10.992	320.670	320.700	100%
	Calzari	2018-01-19	4.685	140.556	138.000	102%
	Diartond	2017-09-01	2.065	103.258	102.200	101%
	Albestros	2019-07-01	1.889	41.568	41.500	100%
	Bartom	2018-10-13	2.353	35.288	39.000	90%
North			5.828	186.820	179.500	104%
	Calzari	2018-01-14	2.718	81.526	71.000	115%
	Diartond	2017-09-05	1.490	74.523	72.000	104%
	Albestros	2019-09-01	925	20.345	22.000	92%
	Bartom	2018-10-15	695	10.426	14.500	72%
	TOTAL		16.820	507.490	500.200	101%

DO

- Sort the data
Alphabetical order is often useless, sort by a relevant variable

- Remove unnecessary grids and colors
Color is distracting

- Use white space to guide the eye
Choosing column widths and row heights wisely

- Use lines and color to emphasize
But don't distract, a gray line or a light color are enough

- Align numbers to the right
And align column titles to the same side as column content

- Mind date and number formats
YYYY-MM-DD for dates, decimal separator for numbers

See the difference? (of course you do!)

The idea is the same as with charts: remove or lighten anything that is not data so that data stands out.

32

Your pocket calculator is Google

There are a lot of slow ways of doing calculations:

DON'T

- Mentally: slow, exhausting, and not reliable.

- Pocket calculator: slow, gotta find the calculator first! Damn, where did I leave it?

- Microsoft Excel: slow, be patient to wait until the program is open and ready.

There's only one way that is quick: Google Chrome's navigation bar.

Open Chrome and type the calculation on the navigation bar (where you'd normally type the web address). Press "Enter" and... *voilà*! Here's your result.

Google supports all the operations you could possibly need for a quick calculation. Here's an example including most of them:

$$((5343 - 4678)/31)^\wedge 2 *80\%$$

Pro-tip: this trick shows its true power when you combine it with the keyboard shortcuts learnt in chapter 4: Alt+Tab → Ctrl+T → Type the operation → Press Enter.

33

Start the day with a To-Do list

The first thing you should do every morning when you arrive at the office is to write down a To-Do List.

"First thing" means first thing: your computer can wait, email can wait. Even coffee can wait.

In this list, include all the tasks that you plan on doing today. The list must be:

- **SPECIFIC:** *"Call sales leads"* is too vague, write *"Call 25 sales leads"* instead. You should also break big projects down into simpler tasks (*"Plan June 1st Marketing Event"* is frightening, divide it into *"Submit permit application"*, *"Place order for materials with provider"*, *"Send out the invitations"*, etc.).

- **REALISTIC:** don't get too excited, there are only 24 hours in a day. Include only a few tasks so that it's doable.

- **PHYSICAL:** leave your computer alone. Write the list down on a post-it or, better yet, a notebook.

Ok, now you have a list. Time to put it into use. Follow these instructions:

- **CHECK IT OFTEN:** 10:30 a.m. already, are you getting things done?

- **CHECK OFF A TASK when you complete it:** it's the prize you get for your effort. Sounds silly? Try it. Soooo satisfying.

- **START FRESH:** a new day means a new list. You can include pending tasks to the new list, but don't just extend yesterday's list.

Managing your time is actually pretty simple. Forget about fancy time-management software: All Hail the mighty To-Do list!

And, guess what? Remember the Weekly Status Report we talked about in chapter 19? Save the daily to-do lists and you'll write it in no time.

DIVE DEEPER:
To-do, to-do, to-do to-do to-do...: bit.do/the-to-do-list

34

Grammarly will help you write better

If you've read and applied all the tricks in this book on how to write well, you're already ahead of 99% of the people.
But there's one last writing trick I wanna give you: install Grammarly on your computer.

Grammarly is an amazing AI-powered writing assistant that will catch all your mistakes and even suggest style improvements. It will make you a better writer. Your texts will shine.

And it works just like a usual grammar & spell checker, so there's no learning curve.

Another thing that makes Grammarly stand out is that it's everywhere on your computer. Grammarly's team went out of their way on integrations. Using Microsoft Word? Grammarly is there. Filling an online form? Grammarly is there. Sending an email? Grammarly is there. You install it once and you get it everywhere. Slack, Twitter, Outlook, Salesforce, you name it.

Oh, did I mention it is free? You can find it at
bit.do/grammarly-app

DIVE DEEPER:
Another cool writing assistant (though less complete and a little bit more inconvenient to use): bit.do/hemingway-app

35

Set a 15-second delay
on email deliveries

The 5 seconds that come immediately after sending an email are terrifying.

These are the moments when you magically notice all the errors in the email you just wrote: an embarrassing typo, something you forgot to attach, someone important you forgot to cc…

If only there was a way to "Unsend"!

Well, it turns out that there is.

Prevent all the "Ouch"s and "Sh*t"s by setting a 15-second delay on your email deliveries:

GMAIL
 > Settings > Send cancellation period

OUTLOOK
 > View All > Email > Compose & reply > Undo

Was your email not ready when you accidentally sent it? Don't worry, click on "undo" and no harm done.

You can thank me later.

Footnote: notice that this is not the same as Outlook's "recover email". This is way better! "Recover email" only works if the receiver hasn't opened the email yet and agrees to let you recover it.

36

Be likeable

That's the final trick, the one that will take you further: be likeable.

Being likeable is actually pretty easy. Follow 4 simple rules:

- **SMILE & LAUGH:** no one likes being around miserable people.

- **ASK QUESTIONS & LISTEN:** people love to talk. Listen to whatever they wanna talk about: their weekend plans, the movie they watched last night, their problems at work...*

- **DON'T TALK BEHIND PEOPLE'S BACK:** if you wouldn't say it to their face, you shouldn't say it at all.

- **DON'T COMPLAIN:** don't be the grumpy guy. We all have petty problems, suck it up and stay positive**.

If you are likeable, your colleagues will like you. If your colleagues like you, your job will be easier. Sam from Marketing will help you build a nice Excel report, Laura from Finance will promptly send you all the cost-of-sales data, Sarah from I.T. won't mind repairing your computer every week and Paul, your boss, will be understanding when you mess up.

There's a catch: for this trick to work, you need to be likeable every single day. A "let's-be-likeable" week won't do.

Fortunately, being likeable is addictive. Try it for a week and you'll be hooked.

in case you were wondering: this weekend I'm going fishing with Dave, last night I watched Interstellar (10th time already!), and don't get me started on my problems at work…

**unless, of course, you are going through something serious. In that case, seek medical advice.*

DIVE DEEPER:
How to win friends: bit.do/win-friends

EPILOGUE

So... now what?

First of all, pat yourself on the back: you made it to the end of the book! That's no small achievement.

But don't congratulate yourself too much. You've read a book on productivity, that doesn't make you any more productive. It's time for the real work: time to start applying these newly learned tricks.

I'm sure you have already applied some. At least you probably installed Boomerang, Grammarly and Lightshot on your computer. That's a step ahead.

But some other tricks are trickier (no pun intended). It's not that they are difficult, it's just that they are easily forgotten.

To make sure that you remember them all, I added a summary on pages 86 and 87.

Focus on five tricks every week and they'll all soon become ingrained.

TL;DRs All the tricks at a glance

ORGANIZATION

TIME MANAGEMENT

INTERPERSONAL

OTHER

37

Extra trick

You thought you had gotten rid of me, didn't you? Not so fast, *Lucky Luke*.

Trick number 37 is a meta-trick. How can you become more productive, when you already became as productive as you can?

By making *the people around you* more productive.

So go buy your friends and colleagues a copy of this book. You'll find both paperback and ebook on Amazon.

I know, I know –what a lousy salesman gimmick. I'm sorry, I'm just a poor old self-published author trying my best...

Did it work?

Did it?

Acknowledgements

Thanks to my colleagues and bosses. I learnt it all from you.

Thanks to Paula, Enric, Roger, Anna and Pau for reading drafts of this book.

Thanks to my family, for always being there.

Thanks to Pep Guardiola for guiding F.C. Barcelona to football glory in 2009 (what an amazing season that was!).

And finally, *you*, the reader. Thank you for your interest in what I had to say.

You rock.

Go out there and get them.

Did you like the book?
I'd love to hear your opinion:

robert.f.basil@gmail.com

And don't forget to leave a
(hopefully positive) review on Amazon!

www.ingramcontent.com/pod-product-compliance
Lightning Source LLC
Chambersburg PA
CBHW021450210526
45463CB00002B/710